Freddie:

A DIARY OF A COT DEATH

Sarah Key is married and has three children, Jemima eleven, Harry nine, and Scarlett, aged three, who would have been Freddie's younger sister. She is a physiotherapist who divides her practice between London and Sydney. In 1990 she treated HRH The Prince of Wales following his arm injury. Her first book, *Back in Action*, has recently been reissued, and her latest book, *Body in Action*, will be published in 1992 to coincide with the BBC television series of the same name.

Freddie

A DIARY OF A COT DEATH

Sarah Key

Mandarin

A Mandarin Paperback
FREDDIE: A DIARY OF A COT DEATH

First published in Great Britain 1991
by William Heinemann Ltd
This edition published 1992
by Mandarin Paperbacks
Michelin House, 81 Fulham Road, London SW3 6RB

Mandarin is an imprint of the Octopus Publishing Group,
a division of Reed International Books Limited

Copyright © Sarah Key 1991

A CIP catalogue record for this title
is available from the British Library
ISBN 0 7493 0796 X

Printed and bound in Great Britain
by Cox & Wyman Ltd, Reading, Berks

To Michele Field

my friend who encouraged me
to speak by the written word

April 1987

Today, five weeks ago was the Ides of March. It was the last day of our son's life. He was ten weeks old.

I found him dead in his cot at 7.45 a.m. on Sunday morning. We were at my mother's house at Newport just north of Sydney, at the edge of the humping and crashing sea. He died in the room which was my childhood bedroom. I knew he was dead when I woke. The sun was up and the cicadas were screaming but the silence creeping out from his room was deafening. There was fear in my mouth as I reached his bedroom door. As I travelled towards him I was led by arms outstretched toward the cot. There was an oddness about the back of his head. His face was buried in the corner of the cot and I knew without knowing that he was dead; the damp hair on the back of his head, the strange pale colour and the aura of stillness around him. There was a muteness, a lack of life which made me stiffen in the anticipation of what I had yet to see.

I bent over to pick him up, but I was frightened to see his face. I turned him around slowly as I took him into me. The under side of his face was squashed but his perfect lips were rosy and wet. I did not even think of trying to resuscitate him. I knew it was not what I should do.

Several times since his death I have been grateful for that: not being given the choice. I was fortunate not to have found him limp and blue with life ebbing away from him. So I didn't feel bound to do something. I was able to let death have its authority. I know I'd be more frightened by trying to thwart death than letting it have its way in peace. To see a child in the last throes must be infinitely more painful than death's porcelain peacefulness.

This feeling of standing back in obedience of death did not leave me, even as his last lungful of air escaped when I picked him up. I knew he was gone and that it was final and I felt a great quiet about it. My initial reaction was to just stay. I felt perhaps that a mother needs a special time to say goodbye before the pandemonium goes up. Then, almost within a millisecond, I was engulfed by my civilised conditioning. 'What if somebody should stumble in upon me!' A mother quietly holding her dead baby as if there were nothing wrong? And besides, there were people to tell. My mother across two rooms, a mile away it seemed, standing at the stove in her dressing gown pouring boiling water into a teapot. I realised how shocked they would all be. And Russell, still asleep in the other bedroom had to hear that his cherished son, his firstborn, had gone. He rose up out of bed like a serpent with a disbelieving odd smile on his face. He'd heard my heavy footfall on the floorboards and he was already alert. With one look he knew. My mother had followed me in; the domestic minutiae of her tea-making ceremony abandoned where it stood. We three just stayed motionless, almost as motionless as Fred. I sat on the end of our bed nursing him and staring at nothing. Russell and my mother stood over me like two guards on duty and none of us spoke. There was the odd, infrequent high-pitched groan from the throat as one of us was convulsed with the realisation. My mother had her hand on the back of my head. She the mother, me the child. Fred was there all right, in my arms. I kept on looking down at him. It was him all right but he just wasn't alive. In death as in life he was lovely to look at. But we were all so stunned that he could have gone like that. How could he?

There was so much time then, punctuated by nothing but dull pain, and I could see that it was going to stretch ahead. I was fitful. Up and down and pacing about with him. I didn't know what to do with myself. Easy to see why people go into frenzied resuscitation activity: they are trying to thwart the finality of death. I didn't want to lie down, I didn't want to go anywhere. I didn't want to stay anywhere. I didn't want to eat. I didn't want to sleep. If I wasn't holding my head I felt best just holding him and looking at him. Looking was almost all I was capable of. Through eyes full of tears.

And then I remembered our other two children (Jemima who is six and Harry, four) whom I had noticed an age before sitting on the floor in the living room. In an uncustomary manner they had been quietly drawing as the raw early morning sun shafted in through the large beach-facing windows, highlighting as it went the dust on the dining table and cracks in the wallpaper.

I put Fred back down in his cot and I called Jemima with me out onto the veranda. I took her by her chubby golden-brown wrists and told her that Fred had died. She had her head on the side looking at me in a sombre quizzical way and then her eyes, those limpid pools of the deep, looked out over the water as if into the universe. I wondered, 'What am I telling her? What do these words mean?', but she probably knew better than I.

Harry seemed less moved by the instant but some time later, as I was lolling about in apathy and the agony of realisation on the veranda sofa, he came to me in silence and laid his head on my thigh. Ah the sweet live flesh! I would squeeze his arm so as almost to hurt him, as I have done many times since, just to see that he is here with us.

Thereafter passed an age. I kept being drawn back to Freddie in his cot. I needed to pick him up and get the comfort of holding him against me; just under the right bosom tightly and firmly against the rib cage. That is where I miss him the most, just where the upper arm would pin him in to my body. How I yearn for the contact.

The other day I drew up at some traffic lights and from the height of my car could see clearly down on to the back seat of the car beside me. We were neck and neck, window to window and there framed in the back seat was the most perfect round baby. It was lying peacefully in its cradle, eyes wide open and alive. I had happened upon him so suddenly as I slid to a halt beside him that I was transfixed. I was mesmerised by the fact that he was alive, half expecting that if I took my eyes off him for a second, I would look back to find him dead. He was quaintly sucking the two middle fingers of his hand, awake but blissfully content. The mother in the front had the blousey bosom of a woman who is breast-feeding and although

I was too high for her to see my face, I felt that she could sense my eerie attention. She was playing with the rings on her hand and kept swinging around as if disturbed by an obsessive gaze. The lights changed and she lurched off in a cloud of smoke. I had a momentary impulse to follow her and explain that my baby had died and that I needed to hold hers. But I realised that I would horrify her. So I let her go, a little brown car scurrying off up the hill, away from me with rattling speed.

Back to Newport and our family loss. It did me a great deal of good to keep going back to pick up Fred that morning. We did not close the door of his room, nor did we offer any reason to the children to go to him or to keep away from him. He was still their brother but he was just not living. An hour or so later, I found Jemima sitting quietly, cross-legged on the floor looking calmly at him through the slats of his cot. As time has passed since, I feel that this has been a help to her. Vanishing, so often synonymous with death, was not the case here and it helped me too.

Then 'the men' came. This was close to being unbearable. Where do you let them take over and you let go? First the doctor, a stranger with a soft middle-European accent, quietly spoken but not wanting to look at us lest he take in too much pain. It was his

Sunday after all. Then the police; two young and burly men carrying their hats; doing their duty by asking the painful questions. 'Where did you find him?' 'What time did you find him?' 'Where were the bed-clothes?' Several times they asked the same questions with me idly thinking I hoped that was what I'd answered last time. I recall thinking that I knew how Lindy Chamberlain had felt.

And then the photographer came. I fretted about this more than anything else. My sister Joey had arrived by this time and she tried to persuade me to go away; for a walk or for a swim. A swim! The first wave would have knocked me down, never to get up. I'd be carried out to sea in an instant, out there beyond, to join Fred.

I felt he needed me there, prowling around with all those men doing things. Oh my poor Fred; having his photograph taken when his face was blind to the intrusion. That cruel popping brilliance of the camera-man's flash dispelling all secrets and exposing the harshness of the truth. Once a photograph is taken the record is there. That he is dead. There is no going back. What happens next?

Thereafter, strange to say, quite a nice time elapsed. My father had arrived and was more upset than I ever recall seeing him. Loud deep sobs and flinging his arms out from the side off his body in anguish and frustration saying, 'You poor kids!' His face was awash with rivulets of tears.

Russell was out on the veranda, sitting on the sofa. His elbows were on his knees and his powerful bowing thighs still looked strong in his anguish. His fingers were interlaced and his knuckles were in his mouth between his front teeth. But I'd got my peace back again. Joey and I were sitting with Fred. He was lying between us on his tummy on the bed, swaddled in his baby-motif flannel wrap. I kept my hand on his back, pressed against him, spanning him crosswise in a cupping grasp. He felt reassuring. He could almost be asleep. I was taking care to keep him lying the way I had found him because by now the underside of his face had become horribly blotchy with hypostasis, where the blood pools in the tissues, and I could not tolerate seeing him like this. I remember saying in a moaning wail as if in reproach, 'Fred, you look so awful.'

I decided that I needed to check his nappy though I never got to the point of changing it. I felt in through the leg-hole; it was wet but not badly so. He was starting to get cold. It is the coldest cold you ever knew; colder than anything else in the room, and now I understand the true chillingness of the word 'chilling'. At the same time his limbs had become a beautiful flawless alabaster, a soft milky cream. His toes looked so perfect, a row of shiny buds.

The next phase was the most difficult because I knew I had to give him up. Through the window I could see two more men coming down the steps. They were peering in the windows of the dimly lit kitchen on the shady side of the house. They hesitated on the last couple of steps and mumbled softly to one another. They appeared to stop and brace themselves, straightening their spines and hitching in their belts before launching into the fray. I heard later that they had just come from a teenager's suicide somewhere else on the peninsula. One forgets that there is tragedy all around.

Somehow I had to manage to give my son to them. How grateful I was to this silent strong man in uniform with his white short-sleeved shirt, when he took him so tenderly. He kept his eyes downcast. I found it such a heavy lift to take him off my chest. Russell and my family were all standing around in a bank behind me in the hallway in silence.

Tears ran down my face but I could see; I needed to see the going of him. The man had several stainless steel pens in his top right-hand shirt pocket which might have dug into Fred's face. I could not allow this

to happen so I took him back out of the man's arms
and rewrapped him so that his face was protected. It
was the best I could do for him. I then turned and
walked away as if to pre-empt the man's turning.

June 1987

Here I sit, three months later, in the deserted office of my physiotherapy practice in Weymouth St in London. I come back here and work for one month a year. It is quiet and messy still, after the hubbub of a busy working day with its constant stream of patients seeking attention and the touch of hands. Cushions are strewn in a disorderly array over the sofa; some are squashed into peaked triangles, compressed by the weight of patients (or us) casually reading the newspapers while waiting. There is a clutter of cold teacups on top of the filing cabinets, chipped and gawdy, as hectic in their ceramic designs as we are in the pattern of our working day. The computer is silent, no hum from its electric engines, inert and opaque for the night. I am tired and delay going home.

London is an empty place for me. It casts me back to the years of working life there with professional success at hand but with a personal life in tatters. I frequently look back now that, for most of the year, I am a comfortable suburban wife in water-washed

Sydney. I recall how I struggled with the anxieties and solitude during that lonely life. Now of course I am lonely in London in a different way, separated from my family and my new baby. There were plans, many months ago, that Freddie should come with me from Sydney as I would still be feeding him.

But almost from the first instant, there were premonitions around Fred. I felt concerned about him through the first night in the hospital, when we were first together as two separate beings. He was so distant. My other children had flopped against me after their delivery, and give or take a few noxious fluorescent lights, loud voices and cold draughts, they seemed just as contentedly oblivious, cradled against my chest, as they had been while being nurtured within. With Fred, it was almost as if his birth was just the beginning of his journey away from me. It was as if he would be staying around for a bit, just to take sustenance and recuperate, because it was surely a torrid birth, but after that he would be continuing his journey. He was committed elsewhere.

Looking back I know that I sensed something. His presence created more unease than joy. I was not worried that I could not care for him, feed him, love him, or discipline him in later life. It was a fear that I could not answer – nor did he expect me to answer –

the dimension of his needs. It was different with the other two; they didn't frighten me. With him, I was out of my depth. I was indefinably juggling with the Big League and I had no idea of the rules. He gave me glimpses into his territory and I was edgy and fearful because I sensed it was different to my own territory. And furthermore, he didn't seem interested in our territory. He seemed indifferent to our life.

For most of the time I smothered these thoughts and turned my face away from the premonition. But I sensed that I was grappling with a profoundness that might floor me.

When I found him that morning, the shock was mitigated by the knowledge that my suspicions had been vindicated. There was no stunned disbelief, I said to myself, 'It HAS happened!' It was by no means a relief, but at last I had been released from some formless dread. Instantly my fear became grief but at least I knew what I was dealing with. It is like the fear of dying as distinct from the fear of death. I have no doubt that death is the ultimate step, the point beyond which all the answers to the universe become known; and when there, there is no need for fear. Fear only accompanies the passage there, whether it be the last few seconds in a plane before it crashes or a mother's subtle sense of her son's travel while he is still with her.

At least death is a known quantity. We know a thing or two about it. For example, there is no coming back. But premonitions, they are eerie suspicions which lie in a different realm.

Soon after Fred's birth I noticed, as if by osmosis, that I could not comfort him. On several occasions I remarked to Russell that I felt I had 'lost the knack' as a mother. He was ethereal and aloof. He hardly ever smiled. From the start his spirit was a wisp of elusive essence, never to be grounded. All the time we had him, he was only a fraction with us. He was preoccupied yet physically fidgety as if he were in a state of preparedness. But he seemed strangely and inwardly discontented, as if his discomforts were not physical ones. I was deeply vexed.

Of course, at the time, none of this was clearly defined. We simply bundled on, I gathered my strength and we embarked together along the journey of the feedings and sleepings. Mothers do a lot of that; getting on with it. While the rest of the family, especially the more distant members, all cluck and coo about the baby and make incongruous observations about who he or she looks like, the mother just plods on. She has got a lifetime with this baby after all, and in a way she is just the perfunctory performer of the essential life-support tasks. She can afford to take a back seat at other times. And besides, they are so closely linked, there is no need for fuss.

One often sees this in the postnatal wards, this remarkable piece of offspring sleeping peacefully in the cot near the mother's bed with the mother either staring ahead of her in times of quiet ward life, or chatting animatedly with visitors. But it is invariably the visitors who do all the holding. It is a well-known phenomenon and the more sensitive mothers have been known to remark upon it, their initial lack of 'maternal love'. It is quite commonplace.

I have often sensed it on their behalf. The mother for the first few days remains at her distance as if she is still bemused at what this small baby has put her through. It is as if the birth process is so momentous yet so determined, so powerful at carrying them both to its inexorable conclusion, that she is meek in its path. Those days before her milk arrives, before she is reassured by the infant's guzzling dependence on her, are a time when she is still getting over the apocalypse of birth.

Maybe the mother is quite overwhelmed by the affair and her confusion is heightened by well-wishers calling her a clever girl. But really, she does not feel clever at all. She feels that temporarily her body was caught in the grip of strange twisting forces. The experience is so powerful and the forces so inexorable that they can be readily misconstrued as the determined will of that baby. And this is what keeps her wary. She is suspicious of the baby's powers. Not hard to see why so many mothers start motherhood with such a lack of confidence.

I was like that this last time. Freddie's birth took so many unfortunate turns, the result of no one major error, just a series of oversights, that I had the feeling that I might die in his birth. Of us two, he seemed the stronger. I had the feeling everything was out of control and that if I did not keep a vigil, something dreadful would happen.

People like me, used to hospitals and outspoken, are unwelcome as patients. Our knowledge, or even intuition, is seen as meddlesome. This often means that we have trouble keeping an audience. My labour was galloping but they were getting it wrong. Deprived of their senses, with eyes only for their gadgetry and equipment, I became more and more frantic with a sense of impending doom. The damage he wrought in making his relentless exit made me frightened of him. I felt apprehensive as I lay there spent and sore on my bed, listlessly watching him over the next several days. My own fear and feebleness in the face of his birth had caused me to imbue him with an equal and opposite strength. A bad experience caused me to be chastened by him rather than to be chastened by the experience.

I attempted to take comfort over the next few weeks in my knowledge that many mothers feel themselves to be impassive at the start. I knew things were a bit attenuated between us but I put it down to my exhaustion and to us both being rather stunned. But shrouded in an indefinable fear I hung back, almost as if I knew that later on he was going to hurt me again.

I saw, since his death, a home video that Russell had taken of us all on the day I came home from hospital. So happy and chaotic we all looked, the wicker crib up on the kitchen table and the doors to the terrace flung open and the sun pouring in. There was a feeling of heavy heat like you get in Sydney in the month of January in the middle of the day. There was the dreamy drone of the cricket on the radio because the English were playing the Aussies. The game had that characteristic sound to it, a comfortable English commentator with impeccable diction, interspersed with short tailored bursts of crowd furore when someone went out. I've never understood cricket but I've always liked the noise it makes.

So there we were in our comfortable chaos with the doorbell ringing and more bunches and baskets of flowers piling up on the kitchen bench. I was sitting outside under the umbrella in the shade from the beating sun and Russell caught me on video looking at my new son as he lay on my lap. I do not remember what I was feeling at the time but it was only after he died when I saw the footage again that it struck me: how I was handling him.

Because I am a physiotherapist by profession, the tools of my trade are my hands. Human touch. I think nothing of grasping a bent and painful human spine in the most matter-of-fact manner. It is second nature to me to take hold with a full-bodied grasp. This will bring the patient along with me; he will pliantly succumb to my handling and if everything goes well, he will get better. But the hands-on is the all important thing; unfettered, unselfconscious skin to skin contact. Wrapping the fingers around in total unharried synergy. The fingers must not be stiff and hesitant; the hands are as one with the problem. If the hands are remote, they will not have it. And if they do not have it, they will not have the cure.

Yet here I was on this day with my own son, making the most artless, ineffectual, dabbling movements with the very tips of my index fingers over his small body.

Yet I knew that this sort of contact from me would lack those essential qualities of comfort and reassurance. I knew also that babies need the full firm contact of their mother's hands; after all, except at times of feeding, it is almost all the contact they have, in contrast to the deep, squashing pressures they endure *in utero*. It was a very 'un me' thing to do. He lay there in my lap, staring up towards me with eyes that looked like pools of dark ink.

I had another garden seat drawn up in front of me with both my feet perched up on the edge so that he rested between my thighs and was propped up in front of me. I sat out there a lot like that with him. He would lay there heavy with milk after a feed, before I would swaddle him and put him back in his crib. Like mothers do, I would sit and gaze at him, exploring his eyes. He always had a funny way of waving his arms about in the air at shoulder level. Funny little aimless jerky mcvements which would resemble a 'go-go' dancer.

But the point is, I was not getting through to him with my touch. My love went glancing off him. I felt that as much as I gave, it got lost in the abyss. A mother knows intuitively if her love strikes home. From the earliest days of life there is a resonance, a return. You sense that in the beam of your love, he is washed in an embrocation that will make him thrive. You feel that the more you give, the more is received.

In Freddie, my love found no home. It went and went. It was like shining a torch out in to the gloom of a starless night sky, spraying an increasingly enfeebled beam about in the emptiness, searching for something to light up. But he was not there and so he didn't light up.

He was unconscious of me and therefore took no comfort from me. He looked past me and he was going there, into my eyes and out into the beyond. He held the secret and his death was the only way of letting me know. It was as if he was attentive to another place as he lay there on my lap. With a bleary recognition, I knew it but I did not dare to trespass. I could tell by the distant way I was touching him. As I ran a finger up the length of his tiny leg it was rather as if I were twirling the delicate stem of a wineglass between my fingers, and with the same distant thoughtfulness.

I am slow to panic but I did a lot of weeping before he died. I was consumed by a strange melancholia. I have never thought of it as postpartum depression because I seemed to know the cause. It was exogenous depression rather than endogenous. Not that all this was nearly as well defined as it reads now. Like so many feeding mothers, these intuitive sensibilities were muddled up with that almost tangible daffiness in the head which afflicts women in the postpartum period, especially while they are feeding.

I was also very aware of this with my first two children. Then as now I felt awash with female hormones which totally governed my behaviour, in particular my powers of reason and logic. No doubt I will be slated by the feminists in our midst, but during this time I felt ridiculously disadvantaged and dangerously on the silly side of being feminine. I was scatty, flopsy and forgetful. I could not have coped with a long-division sum or sat through a meeting on international tax law for all the tea in China. My concentration span was decimated. I would find the wallpaper pattern and the chintz cushions rather more in the nature of my interest.

But this muddle-headedness didn't make me miserable. It meant that I had to spend a lot of time straightening out botches but I also quite enjoyed the feminine hue it gave me. Other mothers were amused. Unlike my career life, I felt I was in an ambit where I could be more readily forgiven my failings. None of this made me sad. My day had no form, it was a muddle from beginning to end, I was slow at making decisions and getting things done, but I operated with a reasonable degree of cheerfulness.

But there was deep sadness on another level in me

and it can even be seen in photographs of me at this time. My latent misery vented itself in cathartic dimension one day when I dropped Jemima off at her school and ran over and badly injured a possum, one of those furry arboreal creatures that live in the Australian bush. It was a mystery how it happened. I had been creeping forward in a queue of cars to the spot where Jemima was to get out. I noticed a wave of consternation pass through the gathering of six-year-olds, all peering under my car. Then one of the teachers looked under too, and obviously pained by what she saw, rushed around to the other side of the car to see what could be done. I flew out of the driver's seat with an almost hysterical burst of anguish. I knew it was an animal and not a child and yet I almost could not bear the way I felt.

The dazed animal was sitting up on its haunches near the huge brutish car wheel which looked silent and dangerous when viewed from this angle, me crouching down low near the road. The possum was quietly using its front paws to wash its face as if it were trying to pull itself together after a shock. It reminded me rather of a fastidious middle-aged woman, self-consciously patting down her hair and straightening her dress having just suffered the most ignominious public fall in the street. The only trouble was that the mess the possum was attempting to clear from its face was blood, relentlessly welling from its mouth and its eye nearest to me was hanging out of its head. It was dreadfully injured.

In a manner seemingly out of proportion to the gravity of the event I became almost apoplectic with agitation. I couldn't imagine what I was going to do to help it. I knew that it was mortally wounded though far from dead. I remember wildly casting about, wondering should I try and chop its head off with a shovel leaning against a nearby shed?

In fact the poor thing, though retrieved by the Wildlife Rescue Service later that day from the rubbish bin into which it was poked by a groundsman wielding a stick, died in agony some five days later, flyblown and infested with maggots while still alive.

I felt miserable about that possum for days and I could not dissociate it from my baby. They seemed inextricably one and the same. Like those clever visual effects of modern cinematography, the two would meld into one, and I would physically shudder. I would look down at the sight of Freddie feeding at my breast and savagely pull him closer to me, wincing at the memory of that possum. And though at the time I did not know it, if indeed they were not the same, they shared the same fate.

Freddie

When I look back on those times now, I can see that I was co-existing with this huge amorphous sadness, this 'something', this strange vague melancholia. I felt my son was slipping me by. I felt he was helpless but I also felt he was unreachable and that I was not meant to try. We were both helpless before what was about to happen and the day was drawing nearer. My joy at having him was tinged with the deepest sadness. I knew he was in all outward ways perfect, but I knew, without knowing that I knew, that he had already left me. The dissolution of the mother–child bonding had already begun.

Late June 1987

Cot death really touches people, especially those you know quite well; those who rejoiced so generously when the baby was born. I find now, here in London, as I do my stint in my clinic, that I am nearly brought to my knees by the task of telling people. Most have been forewarned by my staff before my arrival and they meet me with soft wounded eyes.

I had always been quite mystified if not a little mollified by the enthusiasm and interest which accompanied the birth of my three children. This did not necessarily reflect feelings towards me. Rather a collective appreciation of the joy of parenthood and the love of children. Since I have to admit that I, rather selfishly, had never really been interested in other people's children, certainly not before I had my own, I was somewhat amazed at their 'niceness'. In fact I now see it and appreciate it for what it is and welcome the sentiment as one of the better things that happen as one gets older and starts reaching rosier milestones in life. Babies bring out nice things in people.

Equally so, people are nearly flattened by the news that your baby has died. They recoil in horrified silence and, as my sister Joey related when she had the unenviable task of making the first few flat short phone calls, it is as if you have hit them with a cricket bat. There is something so tragic about the death of a baby that the unanimous instinctive reaction is a tumultuous pause.

After the pause there would invariably follow an interchange the repetitive nature of which set the stage for a strange phase in the bereavement process. The facts were that you had surprise on your side. You knew, as the conversation got going, that you had a horrible shock in store for them. You felt a kind of pity for them, for the upset you were about to cause them. You knew the news would leave them completely nonplussed, fumbling for what to say next. It was at times almost unbearable to watch. But also, it meant that you, the bearer, had to rally inexhaustible reserves if you were both to get over the hurdle. It was incumbent upon you to soften the blow of their impending ordeal.

This took an awful lot of energy and was more draining than any other single thing. Russell and I both seemed to spend an inordinate amount of time trying to reassure others that we were all right, in fact that we were managing. It was a most draining business and seemed to necessitate telling personal snippets of detail that one did not necessarily want to part with at that stage. One instance in particular graphically highlights this compunction to put others at their ease.

It was several weeks after Freddie had died and I had blown up to a size 14 (plus), probably as a result of the sudden cessation of breast-feeding. I needed some larger clothes. I walked into a dress shop where I had not been for a while and the young proprietress looked up welcomingly with a broad sunny smile. I could foresee instantly what was about to follow and I had the very real desire to reverse-wind the film and to retrace my steps back out of the shop and around the corner. She said gaily, 'And how's the baby?' Something made her realise what she was about to hear, her eyes fixed heavily on my face. She saw me hesitate, draw a breathe in and screw up my mouth and cheek and roll my eyes heavenward.

The blood drained from her face and her neck coloured up with blotches of red. Both of us were awkward and embarrassed, ripping at the clothes in silence. The pupils of her eyes were dilated as she looked at me with lasting glances. I purchased more than I really wanted in retribution for the nasty shock

I had just given her and as I was leaving her shop, laden with bursting carrier bags, I said, 'I'm sorry!' Why was I sorry? I was sorry for the hiccup I had caused in her day.

Of course there is always the temptation, especially on bad days, to pretend that you haven't lost your baby at all. Simply to spare yourself the harrowing trial that will follow if you tell the truth. That is fine if you are on the run and fairly safely will not see the person again. But there are almost immediate repercussions of guilt; dismissing him so glibly, simply to spare yourself.

Every bit as inwardly dispiriting is to be asked how many children you have and to hear yourself say, 'Just the two.' A cowardly act. A shutting of the door. Just like hastily turning your back on a problem, on a helpless child, all to smooth out the ripples of life. Nowadays, I will deliberately mark his existence like this, 'Yes, three children but one is dead.' I have found that to deny his presence in any encounter, however brief, makes me feel too wretched. Though he is dead, he still has his number.

However fleeting the interchange, an idle chat with a taxi driver, the manicurist at the hairdressers, the skill, if you call it skill, is to make an acknowledgement in passing. To dwell upon it too long will be to the other person's discomfort. But it needs to be said, and after that I can allow myself an inward nod of reassurance. Then I am comforted by my tribute to him and my feeling of reunion with him.

After the habitual agony of silence, invariably the remark that follows is, 'Do they know yet what causes cot death?' To date it appears not. But I wonder. Surely this is where computers come into their own? Surely in life's rich pattern there exists a welter of statistics which hold buried in them, the key? Is there not some combination of factors which marked his card? Should I not be filling out mountainous pages of question-naires? Was it an infection during my pregnancy? Was I unwell when I conceived? Did I drink too much tea? Did I not get enough exercise? Did I eat something? Did I inhale aerosol spray? Was it the amniocentesis? Was it because he was two weeks early? Was it because he was small? I ask myself over and over again: Where was the slip-up? How can I prevent it happening again?

At this stage, not a day goes by without my scanning backwards and forwards over those pregnancy months like a movie director scanning the rushes at the end of a day's filming. Backwards and forwards they go, slow past a certain point so that I can get a closer view on my carefree and unsuspecting actions.

Did I do anything different there than what I had done with the other two children?

But on the surface, there really does not seem to be anything which distinguished this one from my first two pregnancies. The only two factors which leap out at me are that I had an amniocentesis this time whereas I did not before and second, Freddie was born two weeks early whereas the others were born exactly the day they were expected. He was small for dates.

With so little actually known about cot death it is fairly easy now, as one of the aficionados, to keep abreast of the latest thinking. The list seems endless: a higher incidence in families where one or both parents smoke; a higher incidence in the lower socio-economic bracket; a deficiency in vitamin B1; a baby's raised haemoglobin (oxygen-carrying factor in the blood).

Usually all of these statistics pass me by. They are either inappropriate to our circumstances or defy management from a practical point of view. However, several weeks ago on the front page of one of the Saturday newspapers there was an article which troubled me greatly. Unlike the usual fleshed out pieces of rehashed hearsay, this article was beautifully written, practical and factual. It correlated cot death with babies sleeping face-down.

This article created a storm of unease within me. I could not bear to think of his death being caused by anything so absurdly simple. How could the sleeping position be a killer? (Should I not be arraigned for arranging it so?) The simple sensibleness of the suggestion pierces me to this day, especially in view of the claim that societies which eschew this sleeping position, like Japan, have a much lower incidence of cot death.

I often turn the issue over in my mind and go back over my early reasons for choosing to sleep Fred and indeed my earlier two children, on their tummies. The reasons are all to do with the dangers of inhalation of ingested food. As a physiotherapist I had been only too aware of the dire effects of sucking regurgitated food into the lungs. It is a common cause of death amongst unfortunate alcoholics when they collapse in a drunken stupor and inhale their own vomit. Sad to say, if they do not die from self-drowning, they may do later from the pneumonia so caused. Although breast milk is known to be almost non-irritant in its effect upon lung tissue if inhaled, for me the risk is a hard one to ignore. Even today, knowing now what I do about the perceived dangers of the prone sleeping position, it unnerves me to see a helpless neonate asleep on its back.

Freddie

With cot death, it is thought that lying prone leads the child into trouble by being a starting point from where it can easily drop its head down onto the mattress and smother. This is particularly the case as the child begins to acquire head control. Whereas in the earlier weeks the child is too helpless even to lift its head off the mattress, by about eight weeks the power is there but the endurance is not. You see it rear its head back unexpectedly, as if to take a brief look at the surrounding world and then, as the power fades, bonk!, drop the head back to the waiting mattress.

Funny that I recall that development in my son so vividly. I distinctly recall my fears being assuaged by Fred's first strong though unwieldy control of his head. I even recall remarking to Russell that I felt Fred was not so defenceless any longer. He looked to me capable of putting up a fight.

My pregnancy seemed exactly the same. I never have an easy time of it. I am always sick from the first day beyond five weeks and there was nothing new this time. Like before, I sensed that I was pregnant long before the hormone levels were high enough to test. I had a vague feeling of nausea almost as soon as the first menstrual period was missed and an increasingly dreadful taste in the mouth as if I had been sucking a penny. But as usual the doctors professed seemingly inappropriate delight at these symptoms, saying that the oestrogen levels were healthy and high and the pregnancy was secure.

I do wonder whether I was actually even sicker this last time since I endured the whole pregnancy with an undiagnosed tooth abscess which had perforated through into the sinus above. In retrospect it could have been the cause of an almost constant stream of colds, sore throats, malaise and lethargy which nobody seemed to be able to put a finger on despite countless blood tests and numerous consultations with doctors. It was not until the abscess became painful and I was diagnosed and treated that I started to pick up speed again. But this was only some six weeks before delivery and I was sorely depleted.

The pregnancy seemed intolerably long and debilitating and I tried desperately to find in my own mind some explanation as to why I felt so beaten by it. I had married my husband when Harry and Jemima were two and four years respectively. When we met him I was strong and healthy and carefree. The children caused me no problem – they were well behaved, affectionate and delightful. With the help of various cooks and nannies over the years one could be forgiven for assuming that I handled motherhood, not to mention careerhood, with a misleading sense of ease. One might have thought, therefore, that despite the dreaded morning sickness, I would handle this pregnancy with much the same aplomb.

Sadly this was not the case. From the start I felt behind the start. Probably again because of the low-grade infection of the tooth and sinus, I had a great deal of trouble even getting out of bed in the mornings. Russell was concerned but perplexed that life suddenly seemed to be so difficult for me. I for my part, sensing that I was being such a burden and making such a performance out of simply being pregnant, became more irascible and defensive simply because I knew I was struggling and failing to cope. This was compounded by the fear that at 36 years of age I was really getting on and was even perhaps past it. Perhaps the time had gone when I could put patients through my hands as I did in yesteryear, and at the end of 40 weeks pop out babies of the same quintessential perfection.

There was another strain as well and this was in the form of my book, *Back in Action*. It had to be finished and released. There was a lot of stopping and starting in the later stages with interminable delays and difficulties with the illustrations so that inevitably the publication date in the UK slipped from March to June and then September of 1986. For a long time I had been excited about the book but that excitement was tinged with great anxiety because I knew it would ruffle the feathers of my peers and others in the medical profession. I really wanted to have it over and done with, but that was not to be.

There was always the thought in the back of my mind that this book was taking too much out of me. I seemed to be bracing myself a long way off for the adverse reaction from the profession and it hung over me rather heavily for the whole pregnancy. The fact that the book has done much better than I could have hoped has helped me justify the emotional energy I put into it then, but at the time it was another tide to grapple with.

And so Christmas came and went. Happy days at the beach with much gorging on good food and even some swimming in the surf. Flopping about really; not swimming. Floating about in the tinkling aquamarine waters like a half-submerged shipping buoy. On land, I waddled about getting bigger and bigger until 4 January, when a baby son Freddie was born.

August 1987

I am back in Sydney now and have been for over a
month. How time flies. The weather in London for
my short stint was 'filthy' as the English get some
relish out of saying; it is almost as if they relish rolling
such pithy abuse around on their tongues and spitting
it out. The dear English who have been so good to
me, they save all their overt venom for their disgusting
weather.

At this very moment I am sitting at my Rolls Royce
of a computer as a storm rolls over the bay. There is
the odd flicker of brilliant lightning to pierce the heavy
greyness of the sky and the heavens seem very low.
How I love the electric ominousness of the immediate
pre-storm quiet, such a change from the usual balmy
monotone. It is mid winter and in truth we have had
a filthy day here; the English would be relieved to
know.

Some days having a dead baby hits you hard. This
is one of them. I had a poignant encounter with one
of my patients, a Christian woman with a serene smile

of secrecy and an air of great inner joy. She shyly proffered a booklet wrapped in plastic, something published in liaison with the society for ex-airhostesses (of all things!). It was about explaining the death of a child to other children. So far I have not read it but her manner and her quiet concern touched me. Like all Christians she would have loved to be able to imbue me with her faith, to help me. She spoke with such conviction that it startled me. But I could not rally. Faith did not appear to be coming towards me and I did not think I could take on the search.

But I became mildly rattled that she could see me to be in pain. It is a great guise, in times of distress, to play the role of the healer; to be the strong one. I had taken for granted that people did not see me as floundering. It shocked me rather to think that I might be bearing that face. At that moment, to falter would be to topple right over.

I found that once I had settled her comfortably to relax and optimise the benefits of her neck joints being handled, I didn't want to go back in to her. My throat was tight and I didn't have the strength to be brave. Better to wave her goodbye at a distance as I hurried off to the next patient. But she stayed for a while reading the scrapbook of press cuttings and when I later went back in to the reception area she rose up and hugged me. A shy but strong hug as if she knew all.

This diary shores me up. Yes, London had some bumpy times and I am pleased to be home. Before I went I was mildly apprehensive about seeing the newborn of Debbie, the splendid girl who runs my clinic for me when I am away. She was indeed due to bear her baby two weeks before my planned arrival but was late so that she had only just delivered when I arrived. I had rather hoped the splash would have died down before I landed up in town, not least so that she, her husband and all the girls at the clinic could openly rejoice without feeling they had to hold back on my behalf. Freddie had only been gone three months.

The first encounter was effortless and I was relieved that I seemed untouched. I had determined to make the meeting sooner rather than later, so the day I arrived back in London I saw a few patients and then went straight to the hospital. Immediately I was struck how Debbie had changed. Even though a first-time mother, she had such confidence! For a start, she didn't seem to expect it to die. She seemed so calm; not looking to see all the time. But they were my worries. I would have to grapple with them later, God willing.

But Debbie was so different! What wonders a child does for a woman. There she was, patting her baby's back so authoritatively, as if she had had ten children before. I watched her but she didn't get the creeps and did not notice if I stared eerily. She didn't seem to think I carried some 'vile contagion' which kills babies. I tried to talk normally about Fred and drop his name in as if he were alive. Nothing was said and I understood why. At this point, she needed to ignore his existence. After all she had been through, some three days earlier, she didn't need to be reminded that the fruits of her labours might be lost.

It was not until several days later after that hurdle had been cleared that things got tough, quite unexpectedly. We were all congregated in the office at my practice, a great centre for talking and the taking of tea, of welcoming, of farewelling, of phone-calling and not least of people making repeat appointments and paying accounts. Debbie had come to see us all with Kate, her daughter. Delighted as I was to see her, I was somewhat rattled again by her astonishing air of competence and deftness at being a mother. A physio like me, she has all the skills of handling. Kate could have been bandied around as if she were in a tumble drier and she would not have made a squeak – because her mother was doing it.

It was around 3.00 p.m. and we were all drinking tea. Debbie was joined by a friend and long-term patient who had just had her second child. Both were knee-deep in women's talk about their 'do's and don'ts' of motherhood; the bathing, the burping, the nappies, the potions, the routines. The interchange eternal. The stuff that has gone on through the ages and kept the thread between women strong. I was sitting at the desk behind the computer, listening in rapt silence. The girl had become the matriarch. No wonder the male feels like the wallpaper in those early few months.

I felt like a splat on the wallpaper sitting there, a knob on the computer panel. I realised with a terrible evenness in me that I was not in a position to be able to offer my contribution to the conversation. The discussion going on right there beside me in our milling office did not include me. Even though I had succeeded twice – two were living – the last one had died. Two beautiful children, one of six and one of four, but I could no longer be taken as a reliable source. My recent track record was bad. It was a failure that no excuses could fill. I watched as the silent voyeur, my nose pressed up against the windowpane, looking in on usefulness.

I understood it all, all too clearly. I recalled that

feeling when confronted in earlier days, by the awful-
ness of cot death. In my case, even though my ill-
defined premonitions persuaded me to observe a wary
deference, I still felt it could never happen to me. I
could dodge it somehow. I was a good mother.

This constant tussle with myself, this tinge of
uneasiness, took a turn for the worse many months
earlier, before I was even pregnant with Freddie. I
was dining at a fellow physio's place in London and
another of the guests had endured a cot death. She
was also a physio and in my estimation, not unlike
me. I was unusually plagued by what I perceived as
her sadness. She seemed sensible. How come she
hadn't avoided it? Her loss troubled me. If it could
happen to her, then I was not safe. But even so, I
fought to convince myself that I would be spared. I
tried to persuade myself that there was something in
their air, something in their domestic recipe which
was not quite right. Some fault somewhere. 'They
must have done something wrong which I'm sure I
could not be doing.' I did not want to see her as
someone whose number came up. Because then it
might be my turn. And it was hard to live with it
happening, maybe, to me with the same random accu-
racy. So I knew this was why my friends had to dis-
count me. They were understandable reasons.

But then there was another event. It was a bad
afternoon this. My eyes travelled to the baby's carry-
cot. A capsule they call it. A sheepskin was being used
as the undersheet on which the baby lay. The fibres
of the wool had been combed out so that it was sort
of shaggy and long-pile. On top of this, immediately
under the baby's head was a small muslin square, the
type they (we!) use to catch their little regurgitations
so that the sheepskin does not have to be washed
repeatedly. But it was runkled and caught up around
the baby's face. It looked a bad arrangement. Dangerous. And something that I felt I never would have
allowed. Then it tumbled to me with a sobbing reality,
how aware I had been about the advent of cot death.
It was as if I had been keeping it at bay with one
spindly hand, fingers spread wide apart in a desperate
star, like spanning an octave at the piano with the
tendons standing up against the force. It was something I was always mindful of. I knew it hit with no
reason and the shock would be awful.

I had never been happy to let my children sleep in
their carrycots, always preferring a wicker-walled crib
with its tantalising waves of air flow, wafting through
interleaving layers of cane and across the nose and
mouth of my child. I had also always been fastidious
about tucking in the muslin face-square so that it did

not bunch and threaten to get thrust up in front of the face, obstructing the airways. It caught me so sadly when I became aware of how 'aware' I had been of such a terrible thing happening. I had shown it a respect even before it showed itself to me and I wonder, did I know in my bones, the pattern of my own life? I remembered too with a yank of pain how often I would go and make checks on Freddie while he slept. I recall the sight of him, drawn as I was by some force, to check that his chest was still going up and down. I did this so many times in the ten weeks we had him. Always with his head on the side with his little mouth puckered from the pressure of his cheek on the mattress, I would roughly slip a hand down the back of his wrap, wriggling it under his clothing to grasp his diminutive tender neck between thumb and cupped fingers. This would succeed in shaking some love out of him. He would stir. His eyebrows would go up, his eyelids flutter and he would suck in a breath. A breath like a series of air-sucking drags; three consecutive swigs as he pulled in life. And I would be comforted and creep away. Spared this time? My mind would flick to other things. Many more things to do, rest to get, milk to make before the next draining feed. To think that I had been so mindful all that time and all to no avail. He managed to slip away in an unguarded moment when the vigil lapsed.

My problem now is a sense of failure. After all, I had been ominously forewarned. I have to reconcile myself to having not prevented it. It was this watchfulness that added to my profound tiredness before he died. Sleep which was like a healing drug to me, insidiously transformed itself into my tormentor, so recklessly doping me with perilous abandon. It thwarted the sentry duty and increasingly took on the air of a dangerous indulgence. I would often wake in the darkness with a scrambling start. A reprieve would lead on to the next wearying cycle.

There were times when it would float through my thoughts that perhaps if I were to be the total protector, I should sleep with him on my chest. The natural up-and-down rhythm of my rising and falling chest prompting him obligingly to follow suit. But this was getting too silly for words! I would not allow myself to be driven on to such compromising behaviour. Why should I give in to this baseless fear? The other children had been all right. My lurking panic would pass, my neurosis would evaporate in time. Leave him there in the other room. Get some sleep and get well. Get back your judgement. In the end I was wrong-footed and fate caught me out.

Mid August 1987

This air of foreboding and sense of impending doom about Freddie were never greater than on the eve of his death. The day was full, a Saturday, and we had taken the Hyde Park roller, our lovely big pram, and gone walking, the whole family, around Double Bay, our local village on the harbour in Sydney, to see if my book had come into the local book stores. Unlike usual pram outings, he did not settle well. Instead of being rocked into sleep by the motion of the carriage he was fractious and wriggly. I recall him as pale in colour when we had a coffee in the open air and, big as he now was, he looked too pale.

We then set off on the half-hour trip to Granny's place at Newport with Freddie strapped in between the other two in his safety 'capsule' in the back seat of the car. We interrupted the trip for me to take a look at work in progress at the new physiotherapy consulting-rooms in the city and, again because he had not settled with the motion of the car, I took him with me upstairs, lest he scream the house down while I was away.

He was a trial up there too as I picked my way about, dodging circular saws and paintpots. He had to be jiggered about on one hip then the other to stop him crying and even that did not work for long. I was tiring fast.

We continued the drive to Newport. He may have slept for a small part of the trip but I felt inclined to feed him again almost as soon as we got there in an attempt to start afresh with a feed, hoping that a long cleansing sleep would follow. He slept scantily and by 6.30 p.m. was making noises again.

It was at this point that Marg, one of my oldest friends, arrived. I often wonder in a strange way whether it was ordained that on the eve of our son's death, I was destined to be with two of my oldest friends.

Marg observed me as I went to retrieve Freddie before we set off to Palm Beach. She witnessed me prowling about the cot. It caused her to say the next day immediately upon hearing the news, 'Sarah knew something was going to happen.'

At this point the cot was the simple scene of an extremely bad afternoon of sleep for Fred. I recall looking down at it, vexed. There was a crumpled white sheet with a gay pea-green motif along the top border, overlying a bunched up orange plastic square used to protect the mattress from wet nappies. I spied this hapless orange square with hatred. In my forlorn state I snatched it up from the dishevelled bedding and hurled it hard into the corner, hoping as it went to expunge myself of this terrible disquiet within me. In advance, it seems, I was frightened of suffocation and this dangerous piece of plastic sheeting seemed flagrantly to will on the event.

Before the evening started I was nervy, especially when Harry and Jemima's father rang to alter their prearranged pick-up to go off and spend the rest of the weekend with him. Instead, they were to go the next morning. Russell and I were promised forthwith for dinner at my oldest school friend Chrissy at Palm Beach, at the tip of the peninsula.

I hesitated at asking my mother to baby-sit since she had not six months earlier undergone abdominal surgery for cancer and was barely two months out of needing to be baby-sat herself. And so finally, and also as a gesture at making Granny feel well and back to normal, I asked Chrissy if she could come along too.

Off we all traipsed. One of the many in the long list of 'if onlys'. What if we had cancelled the evening because it was all too difficult? What if Russell and I had gone alone? Left them all in the quiet and comfort of the house we knew so well at Newport? What if we had let them all get to sleep at a reasonable hour? But we didn't.

A distracted and fraught evening ensued. Fred cried on and off almost incessantly. Jemima and Harry were bored, fractious and tired. At one point I remember confiding to our hosts that I should have learnt not to try and do this sort of thing. In so many ways, the mothering phase precludes easy social interchange. Better to take time off and pick up the threads later.

I have never fed my children 'on demand'. I feel that the lack of structure in such a day paves the way in later life for lack of direction and facile recourse to oral gratification at times of need, therefore I will never willingly give in to providing feeds at awkward times. However, Fred was by this time so scratchy, making irritable squawks like a Siamese cat, that again for the sake of peace I fed him.

We were all drawn up at the outdoor table on the terrace. The water of Pittwater was black and at one with the heavens save a tiny tinkle of moon-shimmer as the moon rose over Palm Beach behind us. I could sense that Chrissy was tense. She was trying to rein in her husband Robert, an electric-nervy man with blazing eyes who was winding up to full bore with the Coopers ale. She was failing to hold him in and although he was amusing we were discomforted by her discomfiture.

Again I fed Fred, fumbling around with my dress in embarrassment, trying to avoid exposing a breast veined and taut with milk. Peace descended as his jumpy little body relaxed against me at the table. He drew voraciously from me and I was aware of his black-bright eyes shining at me in the half dark. As he solemnly sucked and sucked his eyes barely left my face. It was the last feed he took from me and I was near to exhaustion.

I then bundled him up with feelings of sheepishness and took him away. We had been a disruption to the evening and I felt we were a polite nuisance. I lay him to sleep on a divan in the entrance hall of the flat.

We did not stay a lot longer that night. Everyone was tired and the night was discordant. When we came to leave and all the miscellaneous shoes, cardigans, purses, car keys, dolls and toy trucks had been rounded up, Russell came to pick up Fred. I remember glancing sharply their way as Russell remarked that Fred was unusually heavy with sleep, 'like a dead weight'. He seemed intoxicated with sleep, barely rousable as his head lolled heavily to one side. We had caught him, I believe, as he was unobtrusively slipping away then. We never knew till later that we had already once caught him in the going.

In single file we all climbed the near-vertical, irregular and unlit steps to the road. The steps were a menace, passing as they went under tangled vines and patches of dripping water. Indeed, it was probably the high point of the night as we all separately shrieked and stumbled and groped, each in his or her own solitary battle with this domestic assault-course in the dark. I recall remarking that if some fictitious floodlights were suddenly to light up, they would freeze me like a spread-eagled arboreal creature clutching at branches and intermittent railings with eyes huge and peering in the murk like a possum. Russell was up ahead on his strong sportsman's legs, bearing Freddie aloft and four-year-old Harry was valiantly bringing up the rear, negotiating stoically steps which came almost up to his knees.

We drove home uneventfully. Russell held Fred in the back. He seemed wide awake and silent as he waved his little bare arms about in the air in his typical 'go-go dancer' fashion. Granny helped by getting Harry and Jemima to bed and Russell helped me as I changed Fred's nappy.

There is not a lot a helper can do in assisting the

doer in the changing of a nappy, especially those of the disposable kind which we always use if we are away from home. But as it happened, how wonderful that his father was there at this last ceremony. Fred lay there abandoned to our attentions, watching us all the while with fixed dark eyes. As if he knew.

I swaddled him tightly in a nursery-patterned pink flannelette sheet and resolutely laid him down in his cot, the end of a long day.

Perhaps it is my imagination after the event, but there was an eerie feel to the air that night as the full moon passed between the dead branches of a gum tree outside our bedroom window; so unlike the scene I am witnessing out of another window as I write this.

At this moment, out in the early dusk I see a kindly neighbourhood boy playing with Harry in the street. They are playing with a neon-green tennis ball and Grant is attempting, painstakingly, to teach Harry the fundamentals of catching. So well coordinated is he, the elder boy some ten years older, as he deftly spins his tennis racket in one hand, the other hand on hip as he stands patiently in a youthful swagger. Harry is off with a yelp, head down, careening helter-skelter into the undergrowth to retrieve the latest miss. What balming, benign normality.

Not so that night. Russell was snoring softly beside me, the noise easily interrupted by coaxing him in sleep to turn over; but sleep was elusive for me. Like a motion picture with stills of the clock on the wall showing the passing hours, I would look up and see the moon advancing in steps across the sky. To this day I shudder, the most unbearable 'if only' of all, to think that at 5.00 a.m., the time I feel sure the last zephyrs of air crossed Freddie's lips, I was awake in the other room with nothing more on my mind other than that I had not slept.

I wonder, I feel sure, that when he died he released me to sink into sleep; that dangerous heavily loaded sleep of the pre-dawn that follows a bad night; that numbing silence of heavy obliterating sleep to blank out the first leg of his journey away from me. How I grappled with that tenacious enveloping burden of torpor as I rose, a couple of hours later, with the screaming of cicadas and the sure knowledge that something was wrong.

And Chrissy's Robert, that wayward man in whom one perceives hysterical snatches of original genius, fleetingly, between the cigarettes and the Cooper's ale, suffered an equally bad night. He too watched the moon go over.

I have a picture he drew. On the day of Freddie's

funeral Chrissy presented it to me. My beautiful Pittwater, which seems to feature so prominently in my
life, with the 'silver shoon' on the water and wisteria
frilly over a pergola in the foreground. It is dated 15
March, the day Freddie died, and the moon is very
low, nearly at dawn. I have this picture hung on a
scarlet wall in my main consulting office in my rooms.
I look at it all the time as I delve around on ailing
spines laid before me.

The men had gone up the steps. I hoped the neigh-
bours didn't see the little figure of sorrow bundled
into whatever it was bundled into. But it was strange
how my mind could not focus and nor did I dwell
upon where he went then. Looking back it was as if he
had vanished. I did not imagine him as being anywhere!

Was it from shock that I ceased to have an ongoing
mental picture of what was happening to him? I guess
I knew intuitively that he was going to undergo a
postmortem but it was a vague notion. I was far from
the mother cat searching frantically for her vanished
kittens; I had stopped thinking. Whereas up until
twelve hours beforehand, not a minute of my waking
hours would elapse without my having intimate
knowledge of where Fred was and what he was up

to, as soon as I turned away from him at the front door, I stopped thinking. It was not until several weeks later, one Sunday night when a barrister friend of ours knocked on the door, that the reality of where he had gone, so defenceless, dawned.

Our friend had been attempting to prosecute someone for the death of a Sydney prostitute, drug dealer, drug addict. As this conversation started, Freddie was the farthest thing from my mind. She was relating how her work had involved her in several trips to the city morgue. I asked her, quite detached, where this place was situated and enquired whether the experience of going there was not too awful to endure; seeing all those dead bodies. It was as if I had back my old-fashioned perspective on death and that Fred's bore no resemblance.

I realised then with a terrible shock that Fred must have been there, in this place I was professing such horror about. I tried to make light of it by saying that I suppose Freddie must have been there at some stage, so it could not have been too bad a place. To my horror, I heard that Freddie had been there while she was there.

I hated hearing this. It was a pain almost too much to bear. I was dreadfully and unexpectedly hurt and felt a resentment that somebody I knew had been nearer to him than I had. It seemed to illuminate the fact that I had not been sufficiently vigilant to find out exactly where on this planet he had 'been taken'. I felt a ghastly neglectfulness. I could not get out of my mind the thought of all those corpses, some with deaths most sordid, all with their name-tag on a piece of string tied to the big toe. Freddie's toes were too small. Round shiny buds of flesh all in a perfect row.

This complete denial came to me as even more strange when I realised how I had made a nuisance of myself, the day after his death, by telephoning the morgue in search of the forensic doctor. It was an experience quite unreal in recollection but at the time I had become almost frantic with agitation. I felt I could not live without the question being answered: had he suffocated or had he just died? I needed to know. I needed some direction. I was thrashing about in an almost ceaseless state of three-dimensional tur-moil. The drugs I had been fed to calm me only served to blot my reason and cause me to perceive distorted proportions of fact. I could no longer live in the silence of not knowing.

Writing this now as the car headlights sweep around the cul-de-sac, some several hours since Harry was out there playing ball, I cannot remember how I found the telephone number of the morgue. It is not as if it is one of those numbers that leaps out at you the minute you open the telephone book. Probably one of those places with a long official-sounding name which belies its true nature. I doubt that it would have been listed under 'M' for morgue, for instance.

But I must have been quite canny. I know I got straight through to where I wanted to get. It was not until the end that I reached the road-block and I remember distinctly the sounds I heard coming over the phone. Rather cheery and industrious, just like the noises one hears when ringing a hospital ward. I can also remember the pleasant sunny voice of the female Pakistani clerk to whom I spoke.

With relief I sensed she was alertly tender but not sorrowful. Expressed sorrow I could not embrace. I had a mission to complete and I could not allow myself to falter. I explained who I was and that I wished to speak to the doctor who had performed the postmortem on my baby. I was quite surprised to be told that the doctor was a woman; equally surprised to be told that the postmortem had already been done. Quite efficient this hall of death.

This exceedingly helpful clerk was obviously grappling to be competent within an aged government department. Instead of having an efficient switchboard, whereby I would have been removed on 'hold' from the scene and stultified by the impersonal tones of muzak, I remained at arm's length as a greedy eavesdropper. I could hear her speaking on another phone, leaving the one to which I was connected down on the desk. The woman doctor was strenuously protesting about having to speak to me. I was hardly surprised; I would guess in her trade she could only remain inured if she kept her distance from the domestic anguish.

My Pakistani clerical assistant battled on tenaciously on my behalf. She had instantly sensed the urgency of my need and tried for several minutes to persuade the doctor to come to the phone to assuage me. The doctor declined. The clerk asked again, couching the request in different terms. She tried a further time; I felt I had a friend for life as I hung on breathlessly with white knuckles and an aching hand. She explained that I was quite sensible and lucid on the end of the phone but that I simply wanted to know if by their preliminary findings they could exclude suffocation.

In particular I had one query: I wanted to know if there was petechial haemorrhaging of the lungs. In suffocation this is caused by the pleural cavity forcibly trying to expand to suck air into the lungs. The dragging effect created on the lungs pops small star-burst haemorrhages all over the lung surface, rather like the tearing effect on a pair of bellows by forcing the handles apart when there is an obstruction of the inlet pipe.

The doctor became more communicative at this point and a babble of conversation ensued. She may have been explaining what I have learnt since, that in cot death cases there is always some petechial haemorrhaging, so that the latter alone is not a definitive factor. I then heard the clerk say in their characteristic clipped sing-song accent, 'Oh! Then it definitely is SIDS, then?'

SIDS. The first time I had ever heard the term; Sudden Infant Death Syndrome. The relief was incalculable but tinged with the feeling, 'Oh! Aren't they kind to me!' Were we all partaking of a tacit conspiracy? 'Don't let's look too closely. Close the book on this. We can't be too sure . . . but in her anguish, let her go.' I smiled. Was it slyly? I was tempted to slam the phone down and get away before they changed their minds.

Mid August 1987

In those first few days people did things for us. Legs of ham arrived, home-made soups appeared on the doorstep. The doorbell rang with flowers being delivered. I could hear the heavy footfall of Ian, my brother-in-law, as he strode purposefully along the hall downstairs. In and out, fetching and carrying for us. He may have been hoping, in the deliberateness of his stride, to pulverise under his heel the misery that clutched at his throat. As if he were trying to banish the feeling; to transform the potential energy of pain inside his chest into the kinetic energy of 'doing'. The catharsis of action. As for Russell and I, we washed in and out of drugged sleep upstairs. The sweetest echo of normality, the ring of Jemima's and Harry's voices floating up from the garden.

My main preoccupation at this point was the pain from my breasts. It could be seen as a cruel stroke of irony that the multiple breast-feeds of the day before had stimulated an even greater production of milk. The pain was indescribable. My night dress was permanently soaked and stuck to the front of me like a wet T-shirt. The bed sheets were littered with inter-circling moons of milk. My eyes and my breasts ran. Comforting well-wishers would look bewildered as I shrank from their embrace.

Brenda, our wonderful house mother and house-keeper, had notified the local Anglican minister of our plight. She is at ease with men of the church whereas I am not. My lack of formal interchange with things ecclesiastical has rendered me shy and discomforted in the company of such people.

He came down to see us and at one point suggested that the three of us pray. We were sitting on the sofa in Fred's room and I felt awkward in the extreme. I felt ignorant of prayer and oafish – an illiterate heathen. So apathetic and ignorant in the past but now scrambling in my hour of need.

I saw my wretchedness in an image of myself: head bowed, embarrassment in the eyes, knees bunched together, feet pigeon-toed. All the while mute and numb, as I played with imaginary calluses on my hands. The evenness of his voice was trying to per-suade me that everything was all right. A kind man he was, not to be vindictive or gloating at our hasty alignment with him, to avail ourselves of his services. I vowed there and then to give this man a chance; to make a deliberate effort in future to swell his congregation. I felt he felt sorry for us that we had no workable faith. He started off the idea of the funeral by asking us what hymns we wanted and I had no idea. The paucity of my repertoire embarrassed me. I could only think of Christmas carols and 'Here Comes the Bride'!

But over a period of the next few days, I began to feel stronger in this strange role. It was our son's funeral after all and I began to feel that I had the right to exert some will over the proceedings. It became important to me that the whole thing was as uplifting as humanly possible. The chill of a young death touches so many people and they needed a fillip as well. The church is beautiful, St Mark's in Darling Point: a thatched roof and walls of sturdy sandstone blocks and highly shined brasses at the altar.

I entered whole-heartedly into the therapy of 'doing'. I rang the florist and ordered masses of flowers for the church; pink roses, gypsophila and gum leaves, bunches not arrangements.

Russell and I spoke to our friend Tim, drawing on his strength to shore up some firmness. He had been instrumental in our meeting and marrying and we asked him to read the beautiful Wordsworth poem at the service:

'Ode on Intimations of Immortality from Recollections of Early Childhood'

Our birth is but a sleep and a forgetting:
  The Soul that rises with us, our life's Star,
Hath had elsewhere its setting,
  And cometh from afar:
Not in entire forgetfulness,
And not in utter nakedness,
But trailing clouds of glory do we come
  From God, who is our home:
Heaven lies about us in our infancy!
Shades of the prison-house begin to close
  Upon the growing boy
But he beholds the light, and whence it flows,
  He sees it in his joy;
The youth, who daily farther from the east
  Must travel, still is Nature's priest,
  And by the vision splendid
  Is on his way attended;
At length the man perceives it die away,
And fade into the light of common day.

Such wonderful words! But we needed his voice to say them.

We asked the minister to contact the Conservatorium of Music to request the presence of a soprano whom we wished to sing the Lord's Prayer unaccompanied.

Back again to the florist to request a bunch of delicate blue flowers, some of which went to make up one of the bunches delivered to the house. This was to be for the top of Freddie's coffin, which the undertakers insisted on calling a casket.

I never did find the mystery blue flower; in a private way I will keep up the vigil over the years to come, casting my eye over pots of waiting blooms in flower shops until I find what I am looking for. The lady in our florist shop couldn't help me. She was bemused, probably put off by my cheery voice; not knowing when to interject and say that she too was sorry about what had happened.

I decided I wanted to wear the bright viridian blue linen dress I had worn on the last night of his life. It was an elegant, uplifting and positive colour and it spelt new life. I somewhat glibly telephoned my friend Chrissy and laid on her the job of finding me a matching wide-brimmed hat with a deep veil.

Little did I know that although she has her own dress shop, she spent an entire day combing Sydney for the hat which was an exact match. It was interesting to note that Joey, my sister, wore a dress that day of vibrant emerald green, another colour of birth and eternal life. Perhaps we both see death as some new rising.

The house started to fill up on the morning of the funeral with friends and family, drifting in on their own errands. Food was being organised. There was chatter and uplifting bustle, homely attention to household chores. I stood in the garden in the March sunlight, watering with a feeble hose.

Brenda brought her daughter's bible upstairs to our attic bedroom during the last few moments of my getting dressed. She had unobtrusively marked a few places for me and the book fell open at Psalm 139. I read it with a voracious breathlessness and was overwhelmed by the beauty of the prose. It was a modern bible, with a minimum of 'thees', 'thines' and 'theretos', which did the opposite of deflect and daunt a novice reader.

I felt reassured and read it over and over again:

> You created every part of me;
>> you put me together in my mother's womb.
>
> I praise you because you are to be feared;
>> all you do is strange and wonderful.
>> I know it with all my heart.
>
> When my bones were being formed,
>> carefully put together in my mother's womb,
>> when I was growing there in secret,
>> you knew that I was there –
>> you saw me before I was born.
>
> The days allotted to me
>> had all been recorded in your book,
>> before any of them ever began.
>
> O God, how difficult I find your thoughts;
>> how many of them there are!

I felt a great urgency to have it incorporated in the service and accordingly got straight on to the telephone to speak to the minister. Sadly, at the time of delivery from the pulpit, it was not the same. It was read in the form of conventional bible language and it was much less moving. Despite this, there was beauty there, buried in the verbiage, and at one point I looked around, half expecting to see people swooning in the aisles at the import of the message – 'The days [were] allotted'. But sadly, in all, it failed to gather us up. Much as I wanted those words to permeate, and the others to hear it the way I had heard it, they did not strike home. The very next week, I went straight out and bought a modern bible.

There were last minute phone calls from the undertakers. I was unimaginably comforted when it was explained to me that Freddie was coming in the car that was to pick us up. It was as if he had come back to us! He was picking us up! He was still dead but he was coming to get us and we would all go together to church. It was even more comforting that he didn't arrive in a hearse. Just a long black limousine with no outward signs of death. And there, if one bent over and took a peek inside, there he was. The diminutive white box, facing frontwards. It was covered in rather unattractive crimplene embossed stretchy cloth and there was a small stainless steel plaque with his name etched on it. Frilly writing with curlicues, but it marked his presence.

The coffin was positioned in such a way on the back seat that Russell and I rode to the church sitting either side of it. We rode in silence, both resting an arm along the lid of the box and we both experienced our first moments of acceptance and tranquillity. Our backs pressed into the back of the seat as the car pulled up the hill. I have wished the ride was longer; wherever we were going, it was nice to be going together.

The day stretched long into the night. They all stayed on. For a lot of them it was as if they didn't know what to say so they just wanted to be there. Some friends only spoke to me once they had floated into drunkenness and I knew that there were many who were knotting and unknotting their handkerchief before they talked to me about it. Russell's sister came up to me on her way out. Her head was turned self-effacingly to the side, she shrugged her shoulders and gesticulated mutely with her hands as her arms lay at her side. They all felt they had to 'say' something and I was touched by their compassion. Addressing the problem square on. One by one they made their peace with me.

I have a mental picture of Brenda standing at the kitchen bench, head bowed all day making slabs of bread covered with chunks of ham or salmon. All day she seemed to saw away. Her gentle tribe of children quietly threading their way between us all, offering plates laden with food. The wine ran and the more it slopped, the more people began to feel better. It was a Wednesday and I could not get over how people seemed happy to stay.

Earlier, Russell and I had gone off alone with Fred to the crematorium. The minister accompanied us in the car. I remember feeling struck dumb in the car, again with feelings of tangible hypocrisy at being in the company of this man yet at other times seemingly having no time for him. At least at our wedding, where more latitude for planning was permissible, we had married on my father's boat on Sydney harbour.

He guided us along as if these things are a normal part of life and we gathered confidence. At the crematorium, Russell asked to carry Fred to the altar. He walked up the central aisle with his shoulders squared and jaw set. He was trembling and his face was ashen. The two of us sat in the front row of this cheerless, tiny chapel with windows made of glass the colour of pale beer bottles. It was the most desolate of places, about as inspiring as a bus shelter.

In complete contrast to the church, the crematorium is devoid of faith, a flimsy modern mausoleum built around a conveyor belt. Its smallness is chilling, as if to mark the bereftness of the modern family unit. Its architecture is in keeping with its perfunctory farewell performance; a confused and glum ritual for that bedraggled knot of people who hang around after the ceremony, talking in whispers. It is over so quickly that they are uncertain when to leave. So they hover. The high heels of the women dig into the manicured lawns. In time, they drift off to their cars, exchanging muted farewells and wan smiles. Car doors bang, engines roar, gravel squelches under car wheels and then there is silence. Just the birds and the building and him inside.

It was the same chapel to which I had been almost five years before, to the ceremony of another cot death baby. Jemima was a round cherub almost one year old and she cooed and gurgled softly in her pushchair as she played with my sunglasses. Being in Sydney on one of my flying visits from England I had poor baby-sitting facilities and had no option but to bring her along with me. For many months after I agonised that it had been inappropriate to have my child there when this couple had just lost theirs. Her precious guttural gurgles interleaving as they did through the drab tones of the preacher in the pulpit seemed to say that there was hope again for them, in time; but they had also seemed to say that there would be a deafening silence in their home that night.

We returned to our home. As we pulled up, Jemima and Harry were running around in normality mode, gorging themselves on food and enjoying the adoration of all the adults. In our absence, Marg and members of my family had met and welcomed people at the front door. By the time we arrived back, some hour and a half later, friends were bulging out of the place at every opening. I was so relieved to see them. We needed company. Russell put people at ease by casually taking up the role of host. But nevertheless they needed a sign from us that we were coping. I remember as we entered the room, I threw my hat and dark glasses off into a chair and said, 'Hi everybody!' And Russell filled their thirsty glasses.

Late August 1987

It is 4.00 p.m. on a Friday afternoon. Harry is playing in the cul-de-sac with Andrew our neighbour and Jemima is sitting here beside me writing dishevelled looking rows of 9s and 13s along faint-ruled lines. She is so pretty with her glossy grey-brown curls and her clear wide eyes. How enchanted she makes my life. I keep breaking off and leaning across and passionately biting her cheek. She thinks I am mad. I always bite them when caught in exquisite paroxysms of parental love. I remember in a shop once when Harry, with bored and frustrated resignation after being motheringly nuzzled, directed me in clearly audible tones to stop biting him. We got many quizzical glances from the crowd. Perhaps they'd think it's usually the child that bites . . . What would I do without them?

Parenthood has helped me a lot. It has helped my confidence. You lose a large helping of confidence when you lose a child. Indeed, at the moment there are times when my sense of confidence and sense of safeness are so shaken that I feel I am a walking acci-

dent looking for somewhere to happen. I no longer
feel protected by an inviolable buffering field, that
intangible attitude begot by ignorance and lack of
touch with calamity.

Like many I see around me still, I used to have an
air of sureness bordering on complacency. I always
felt I was quick-footed enough to avoid disaster. And
I am sure my conviction occasionally did deflect disaster like the muscle-man in the comic strip rebuffing
gnats off his chest. I only had to look it seems, a
confident sweep of the gaze and danger would wither,
craftily shrinking back in wait for some other passing
aura, more pervious to its mischief than I.

At the moment I am the target. I am down on to
one knee. I am barely protected at all. I am no longer
impervious to shock. I am experiencing what the aca-
demics, it seems, have already described, 'life's hap-
penings are clustering'. I have developed the aura of
a victim and things will happen to me.

Like the panel of convicted criminals who (I recall
in my fount of useless information) were shown a
snatch of film of people in a crowd. They were asked
to observe closely the faces they saw and then to iso-
late those which they would most readily choose as
victims to bash and steal from. Astonishingly, or not
so astonishingly, the would-be assailants all identified

the same hapless few. Perhaps those that were half-broken already, emitting a telepathic message that they would be a pushover, receive the violence and offer minimal resistance.

Is it a depletion by grief of my own energies that causes me to feel that other disasters are about to attach themselves to me? An equalisation of the planet's rampant forces? Force and aggression targeting a vacuum? At the moment, this is me, offering no resistance. No longer like the child's toy with lead weight in its base so that it bobs upright repeatedly after being knocked. Unthinkingly confident and indomitable it lurches back upright after each vexatious blow, all because some basic laws of physics have made it impossible for it to remain toppled over, disabled, on its side.

I have always listened with wonderment to my elderly patients who seemingly live in dread of falling. It is as if such an event will mark the end of their life. They seem to totter on the edge of disaster, courting it every time they step out of the front door. A fall seems to take on new significance in the minds of the elderly. Sad to say, I often felt a type of aloofness in my compassion for them, since a fall had always been such a rare event in my own life.

No longer. Because now I am falling. At the moment

the trivia of life have become the trauma of mine. And furthermore I am receptive to disaster, meeting misfortune well in advance of the healthy halfway point. I no longer move easily between the furniture, I am clumsy, I trip on paving stones. I bang my precious hands. I attract ructions. I have become one of those people that awful things happen to. Some days I feel so vulnerable that I am nervous crossing the road. I could so easily fall.

I now see that falls beget falls; once down a fall becomes one of many.

September 1987

The first day of our spring. A day feeling stunned in the head and jaded after an hour and a half of talk-back on a radio show, late last night. Thousands of listeners, a blur better not comprehended and a swarm of questions hurtling at me out of the black of night. I've done it before but I have the feeling of bringing myself up to the line as never before. The adrenalin causes a breathy thrumming in the microphone as I lose control of my breathing as my nerves wind me up. There is a furious sense of immediacy as I wrap my mind around the next and the next unrelated query. The focusing is mind splitting as I toy with my earrings, opening and closing the clasp over and over again on the bench in front of me.

With 20 minutes to go I looked over at Owen who works well with me and protects me from unintelligible questions from desperate bodies, alone and awake in the middle of the night, and it occurred to me that I have been there with this. I am running out of steam. My book, my precious surrogate thing to pour my passions into, my 'baby' which swooped down and rescued me so quickly after Freddie, has done its dash. It was a tumultuous and exhausting ride, dogged and focused, to take me away from the immediate pain. Now with the first day of spring, as I stare out of the window with hollow eyes, I see the small tufting sprigs of green of the grape vine. I am listless and spent at the dawn. My host played me 'Goodnight Blinkie Bill' over the air waves as I drove home after 2.20 a.m. and the radio show went on.

I do not need the book any longer. It has its own merits. It answers a need and I am relieved. I'll let it go now. A sleeper quietly getting bought and sold all over the country without my ever knowing about it. I'll let it speak for itself.

I wonder if people looked askance. Did their eyebrows go up? When I so quickly rallied and threw myself into the publication of my book. Yet I remember the fear of the media and the launch acted like a kind of counter-irritant. The loss of Freddie left me with the feeling that I wouldn't be so easily frightened any more. I launched into the fray with a kind of impervious disregard, a flinty resolve. My nerves had already been steeled.

I would walk and work with my sorrow held in. My lack of talking about it would strengthen me. Give me any task, any other task, and I'd knock it over. I would recall, when centring myself for another tangle with an interviewer, with the second-hand sweeping around the clock on the wall, nothing can frighten me now. Nothing like the fear that was in my mouth the time we went to see him at the undertakers.

It was two or three days after Freddie had died. A strange time. So much space for thinking; the rest of the world in limbo. We had both been lolling around, flaccid, in a phase of subacute grief, feeling stale and dispirited. It was weird the way the unexpected grief waves would hit you, 'I've lost my baby!' Immersed in it all the time, like bathing in the surf, ducking under each roller as it makes its way in toward you and towards the shore. Like the encounters along the way, you could see them coming and you could gird yourself for action – only to find yourself knocked over by a backwash from the beach that you weren't expecting. A cold shock of reality. A good cold dunking in fresh raw pain.

The visit to the undertakers was worse than this. I had begun to fret at losing touch with that peace I had derived from carrying him around so much after I had found him. The good samaritan from SIDA, the association which reaches out to bereaved parents, had called to see us and she assured me that I could see Freddie again if that was what we wanted. It was arranged. It was the first time we had been out since the day, I recall it seemed bullish and torrid out. Everything, the sun, the noise, the traffic seemed menacing. Then I realised that the hurly-burly of life goes on.

The undertaker's waiting room was furnished muted-modern with low foam sofas covered with maroon velvet which were hard to scramble out of, so that your knees flew apart. Muzak played, a chirpy tune in the background. A pretty girl was typing in the reception area. 'What can she be typing?', I thought. Something to do with death. I secretly admired her for working there. It can't have done much for her social life in the first light-hearted interchange. We sat there for a while, watching the office life go on, while they were dressing Freddie. We had brought clothes for him to wear. Periodically someone would come in or go out, and the automatic doors on to the street would glide open. We would be startled by the sudden roar of the traffic outside.

I was beginning to lose my nerve and I was right; I wish now that we hadn't seen him. We were summoned by a deferential man who called us with his eyebrows, hands clasped. I felt shaking fear as we walked along the passage to Freddie. Nothing could frighten me after this.

One of my closest friends in England also suffered a tragedy with her three-year-old daughter. She was drowned in the swimming pool into which she fell, before the rest of the household had woken up. Torunn my friend was in America at the time so she saw her dead child for the first time in the mortuary. She felt greatly comforted the first time but not at all the second. I remember her saying that her child was like an empty husk the second time, as if her spirit had flown.

The same was true with Freddie. What is more, this time I was deeply frightened of him: that he was cut up, and with a bonnet and clothing hiding the incisions; a bonnet that he never wore. And also that he was cold. Too cold to touch. Russell and I hovered over him, peering in at him as he lay in a crib with nylon flounces around the edge. His face was unrecognisable, and wearing that absurd hat! I put my hand out to touch him but Russell took it away. He was isolated from us now. We were voyeurs staring at a departed person. We didn't dare to touch him lest his garments fall askew and reveal some dreadful gash with stitches. That last cuddle that I yearned for, pinning him with my right arm, like a wing, pressing him against my chest wall, was not going to happen. The room was incredibly dark. No artificial lighting, with one dingy window heavily draped in shrouds of tassles and curtains. So unlifelike. We wrenched the curtains back and tied them ingnominiously around themselves, to clear a way for the light to flood in. But the light that fell on did not bring him any closer to us. He looked different, gone. We shuffled out. 'Thank you', we mumbled numbly, tripping over each other's heels as the noiseless doors slid open and the traffic on the street roared.

November 1987

I often try and dissect out dispassionately what it is that I feel having lost my baby. Is this, I wonder, what all the professionals call 'coming to terms with grief'? I can clearly state that there are fewer things more enmeshed by clichés than death.

As far as coming to terms with his death, I feel my acceptance was almost instantaneous. There is nothing more final. There is no mistaking it when it happens. Quite quickly things flow over your mind; you see that there has been no violence. Just alabaster and uncontactable. Stopped. As reasonable as a clock stopping, tick-tocking no more.

I have said before that I sensed that I was going to lose Fred. Sometimes the sadness of him repels me, even today. There is one particular photograph in a frame which I keep meaning to remove. I cannot remember when it was taken, perhaps it was after a period of anxiety and doubt so often experienced with him. I wonder what it is that goes on troubling me; just this one photo. He looks sort of mute and only half responsive. It was as if all our smiles and cooing attention overlay a chasm of pain.

Today I look the train home from my morning's work. While I sat on a seat, thinking my own thoughts in the windy tunnel, a baby's wail rang out above the gusty rumblings and clatter of miscellaneous feet. It was a piercing sound that wail. I was moved to recall the often quoted statistic that a baby's cry has proven more rousing, and in effect harder to ignore, than any other sound known to man. What mother will forget the thumping sense of unease, being woken in the night by those snuffling sounds of melancholy? I recall so vividly the early hospital nights when I would wake, almost with a sense of panic, and I would fly out of bed to gather up my crying child.

This sense of agitation is indefinable yet undeniable; an instinct propelled by unreasoning fear. At those times, you have the sense that nothing else is important and that you simply must be there. The ultimate anxiety of course is that your baby is dying, a mother's greatest blow. This is a troubled and deeply buried suspicion, especially in the early days of your child's life. You have cleaved off this tiny living thing and you feel that sleep and other abandoned moments are stolen back at your child's peril.

And it is this panic, this innate fear of stumbling in

on death that terrifies me. Funnily enough, sitting down with death after the discovery is the calm in the eye of the storm. A respite from that ill-defined, repetitive and fateful galloping anticipation of death.

The trip to him took an age; slow motion. Dressing gown trailing out behind me, painted toenails over the floor boards, past the seashell door handle, over toys, dodging the furniture. The children with their necks craning. The door opens with a popping sound (by the sea all locks corrode) and Freddie's cot and the back of his head loom up over the horizon at me. I too am asphyxiated.

'Oh! My God it has happened.' When I lifted him up, his tranquillity and the irreversibility of that state set me free. A far cry from that painful surge, the drench of the adrenalin as it floods the veins in the dead of night, only to be assuaged by the silent nurturing bond of skin to skin contact and feeding. The gulping down the gullet of life.

My mother relayed to me a strange question from one of her friends whom she had contacted about our Fred's death. She was asked if I screamed when I found him. Screamed!? Is the poor woman mad? This oddly obtrusive question made me realise how frightening it would have been if I had screamed. I would have frightened myself and made this precious final time ugly with the violence of bereavement. Thank God for the peace of it.

March 1988

It is almost a year to the day that Freddie died. We, the four of us, have just returned from lunching at Kings Cross, the checkered heart of Sydney. Jemima has tomato sauce smeared all over her face and new teeth appearing at all angles and Harry is tearing about in the garden at breakneck speed. He has a pair of jeans on which are slipping down over his little apple bottom and a pair of over-sized trainers that he would prefer to die for rather than part with. A quick spate of afternoon gardening – or rather sweeping of early autumn leaves – followed by some thirst-quenching drinks for the window boxes, and now here I sit with the window thrown wide open and the aroma of wet earth floating past my face.

Back to this time last year. Few things rattled me really during this oddly painful time. I did not cry voluminously. I would only cry if I was caught off balance; having to explain it again or seeing a documentary on television of a premature baby fighting for its life. Most of the time I felt as if one arm was missing and I was getting used to being without it. The first thing that you notice in a practical sense, is how much time you have. There is such a gaping vacuum of nothingness left; a void in place of comforting domestic clutter. No more nappies. Discarded toys or baby artefacts (baby singlets in the wash, or wraps) lying useless around the house. Silence and inactivity in place of the helter-skelter routine. It is no wonder you have so much time for mulling over your misery. You compare what you would have been doing this time yesterday, this time last week, last month, last year – perhaps it was before you were even pregnant, let alone before you'd created another life and lost it. You marvel at your previous usefulness and how you rode so confidently before the fall.

The collecting of Freddie's ashes was one such incident where the ugly disadvantage of misunderstanding caught me so off balance that I thought I was going mad. It was some several weeks after Freddie had died. It was perhaps the most miserable time for me. The shock was fading but not the sorrow. You might call this the subacute phase; I think for most people, it is the worst. Inevitably, you begin to feel that the support is waning. 'Life goes on'; people resume their lives. And you, you have to get on with it too. Several times I had a slightly panicky feeling that I could wallow in the trenches forever. How often do you hear it said, 'Poor girl, she never got over it'? There weren't many times that I felt this bad but the matter of the ashes brought it to the fore.

I worried a lot after the dreary little cremation service that he hadn't 'gone' there and then. I didn't want to imagine him waiting in queue, one little white coffin wedged in between all those dark monsters, most of whom had had a good innings. I needed him to be rendered 'earth to earth, ashes to ashes' instantly upon his rolling out of my view.

The ashes were not available immediately. I didn't want to make a return trip to the crematorium so we were to be notified when I could pick them up in the city. A long time, maybe weeks elapsed before we were contacted and I set out one day after work to go there.

The address was in the heart of choking inner Sydney. But I couldn't find the building. The number was in an obscure place so that in the first instance, I walked straight past it. I didn't like walking past him, not again. I stopped and gathered myself and quelled the feeling of rising panic. I retraced my steps, walking deliberately, and counting the buildings from where I had last seen a number. I found the building that had passed me by and I remember staring up at it reproachfully as it loomed its impassive bulk up into the airy blue. Still with a head of muddled confusion I went inside. The ground floor was dimly lit and the sounds of footfall of the workers rushing by made a high-pitched echo on the ringing marble.

I didn't know what I was looking for. This didn't look like the sort of place Freddie should be. Was it a funeral director's? Or cremation people? What sort of name did these death specialists go by? I imagined that whoever they were, they were on the thirteenth floor.

The doors slid open noiselessly and I was greeted by the bland furnishings and the muted tap-tapping of a nondescript large city office. There was, again, no name on the wall so I walked up to the bland, again, receptionist sitting at her post with her legs quietly folded at the ankles and I asked her if this was the city office of the funeral director's.

The empty and expressionless face of this woman looked at me. Slowly it changed to become one of mild humour mixed with distaste, even tetchy indignation as she squirmed on her seat and turned her nose up in the air. I suddenly felt on the verge of uncontrollable tears. I had the wild suspicion that I was the subject of an outlandish joke. A conspiracy to keep me from being reunited with my son and all these uninterested and barely human people were the bit-part actors in the scene.

I withdrew instantly back to the lifts and waited an eternity for another to appear. I needed to be enveloped in an elevator-pod to be taken away from this place. I remember feeling hunched at the shoulders with a stinging ache between my shoulder blades. I felt I didn't have the strength to stay in the building. I would flee and try another day, with the confidence begot of equanimity.

In the foyer again I was relieved that nobody appeared to notice. No sideways glances. I could stand back and lean with a swagger against the far wall, its cold seeping through my coat. I could wait till my breathing returned to normal. I could look over the heads of the people rushing past and peruse the list of tenants. I could take as long as I liked to find the name that only I knew I was looking for. There was no funeral director, only a cremation service, and not on Floor 13.

I called the lift again, ascended to some other place and left the building some time later with a grey plastic box in my handbag.

But there the tale does not end. I had planned, immediately upon returning home that day, to scatter his ashes with joy over the garden all around our house. He was going to be back with us and all around us. I was itching with excitement to do this, to feel him mixed with the bursting trees and in months to come, to be emanating in the form of scent from luscious blooms of the garden flowers.

But again I was thwarted. This box was impenetrable. It had a hard heat-sealed rim around the top edge that defied, with all the best fingernail-tearing activity, being opened. Despite any amount of prizing and levering with a multitude of knives and other objects, it could not be opened. Again I had the feeling that I was being kept at bay.

Again I felt that I was being watched, this time while doing something appallingly sacrilegious. A demented mother, violating her son's grave. My fury and tearful frustration gave way to meek submission since I felt I could not ask anybody to help me. Furthermore, I could not subject that box to the smashings of a sledgehammer, which we don't have. So it might have to be a plank of wood or a huge rock from the back garden, and imagine that for a bad scene! One skittering shiny plastic box lying in the dust, being pelted and bombarded from all angles by sticks and stones, the heel of a shoe or the massive wheel of my car in the driveway. Who could indulge in such symbolic persecution? I couldn't. So there to this day it sits,

Freddie

Freddie's ashes on the dressing table in Freddie's room. A real life conundrum with the answer floating in the balance until I can muster the courage to telephone the awful cremation people and ask them what they are playing at.

What an absurd idea they must have of death to attempt, as they seem to be doing, to prevent those ashes from re-entry to the world and joining life's cycle. What did they expect? Did they imagine that we were going to wall them up in a hole in cement somewhere for some later civilisation to unearth and kickingly discard with the rest of the rubble? No wonder there is so much fear of death.

In some ways I am not confident with this death business and I am left with the feeling that it is I who am behaving improperly. But I am quite happy about him sitting up there upstairs really. It completes the room and it is *his* room after all. At least if the cot sits there, empty and inert in the far corner, Fred is still in the room.

April 1988

There is new life within me; it didn't take long. Twelve weeks on, six centimetres long. Technology shows me a recognisable head and muscles covering the limbs. Despite the ever-present morning sickness there is magic afoot.

I have the prescience that this baby is a little girl; I do not feel as unwell as one does while carrying a male child but perhaps this is the thinking of a wishful mother. Two thirds of cot deaths are males. Of course the all-pervading presence is that IT could happen again. Could it really?

There was a fly-on-the-wall documentary the other night on television, all about homebirths. How flagrantly wilful those adults were, wanting everything to be 'nice' by insisting on having the baby at home. I was troubled by it, not least by their astonishing lack of modesty. The women convulsed in sweaty pain on their Berber-carpeted floors with all their knick-knacks on the shelves behind. How hard the labour looked;

I was quite wrung out. But it was the newborn that transfixed my attention.

The sureness with which they push on out. When they arrive they look squashed and stunned. I watched as I had done with my own, that characteristic rolling and squinting of those unseeing opaque eyes. The peculiar involuntary movements of their fingers, widely separated so that the little hands resemble writhing star-bursts. They looked, and plainly are, incompetent to survive unaided in the outside world, yet to have survived that journey? You would think they could survive anything! Why is it then that some inconspicuously slip off later on?

I have my own home-spun theory about what happens. It is all to do with the sucking reflex. I believe that my baby's sucking reflex was too powerful. I believe this co-existed with a breathing instinct which was conversely weak. I believe that in the circumstances of death, the desire to breathe, being weak was overwhelmingly disadvantaged by the much stronger instinct. And perhaps simple tiredness too played a part, but the end result was that he sucked rather than breathed.

Freddie was a great eater. He loved his food with such a passion that I found it hard to keep it up to him. He was a small baby, only 6lb ½oz and he was also born two weeks early. Both factors made him eager to catch up.

Almost as soon as he was clear of my loins his mouth was working, gulping at the air like a goldfish, the reflex making him scan the universe for sustenance to take in. I was initially thankful; having already had one child who was a feeder and another who was almost apathetic about food, I was only too aware of the easy passage ahead with another easy eater.

However, unlike my experience with my earlier two children, I was aware that my supplies of the super-rich colostrum were becoming inadequate to tide him over until the milk came. In the past I had barely been aware of this two- or three-day interval, but this time I was counting the days. He seemed permanently hungry and in need of more, sometimes half an hour after his last feed. I was comforted to be told that Freddie had been born small and that until he achieved his genetically preordained birth weight he would feed and feed and feed.

This was certainly what he did. He thrived. His weight sky-rocketed over the next few weeks. But although his feeding pattern evened out and his demand became more regular, he still maintained an astonishingly overactive sucking reflex. Most of the time he was automatically nuzzling and attempting to latch on. Anything that brushed past his lips or cheek he would immediately turn to feed from. In his short life he was a complete slave to this reflex. Anything within reach he would nuzzle and worry until it became sodden with the wet from his mouth. I would find my collar wet if I had been holding him vertically up by my chest or his blanket-wrap damp if it passed close to his face. And if he was close to my face, I could sense the urgency with which he pursued this innate drive.

This never worried me unduly at the time but I unearthed after his death a photograph. Fred and I were on the bed; me exhausted again, looking like a wilted lily; Fred lying beside me, swaddled. But the ominous detail was that his face was pressed hard into the surface of the mattress. Just like a child puts down a doll with its face totally buried from view. Except that Freddie was different, he was engaged in a frenzied search, looking for satisfaction in the increasing wetness.

In retrospect I remember that I was aroused by whimpering and snuffling noises which were not alarming in themselves except that they seemed to be going on for so long. They disturbed me rather like one worries about a dog chasing its tail. My feelings were more that, 'He's at it again and should be stopped.'

These days, my daymare about Freddie's death is that this is the picture of his final moments. I worry that he nudged and nuzzled and sucked at the mattress until he died. That despite the urgent ringing of alarm bells as the oxygen levels dipped lower and lower, his instinct to suck was too great and won the day.

Upon finding him that morning, there was a large circle of wet, much wetter than damp, on the sheet under his head. Answers to my queries suggested that this was drooling from his mouth after he died. This I do not accept. They would have to have been there to see the soakingness of it; it was almost the circumference of his head. Was it not the result of a cruelly misdirected primitive reflex? A reflex which had been activated at birth because he was born small but one which persisted, through a peculiar quirk of nature, beyond its call of duty and became deadly.

March 1990

We have just had the anniversary of three years since Freddie died. For the most part, I never seem to think of the age he would be now. I seem to blot out that sort of detail. To me, he will always remain the age he was. But there is one child whom I find too painful to see because he is the age Freddie would be. They were born two weeks apart and we have photographs of his mother and I, feeding our babies in the back garden. They lived nearby, with both fathers in the same profession and it was discussed in a casual sort of way that our sons would probably do lots of things together in life, like going to school, playing cricket, breaking our hearts at the same age and so on. Afterwards, inevitably, we drifted apart. The other family spends a lot of time in the country and these days our paths rarely cross.

About a year ago, I was in my local shopping centre and I became aware that a woman was approaching me in a determined fashion, on the footpath, waving. She held the hand of a small blond boy. As they drew nearer, I felt an urge to turn and run. I was ill-prepared; I felt breathless and paralysed in reaction. I tried to talk to her but I was lost for words. It was difficult; my brain wouldn't work. What could I say? I had to force my eyes away from his face. He was so perfect. Little socks and shoes and neatly pressed shorts. Blond floppy curls and baleful eyes staring up at me. He was walking and growing and calling her 'Mummy'. We were embarrassed as my eyes filled with tears and I tried to pass it off, scrabbling in my handbag for tissues. There was nothing I could say, so I had to leave, withdrawing by walking sideways. Sadly, I think she felt wretched too, but what could I do? Not make another date to see her for tea and spend some more time staring at her child.

But by and large life gets easier. Funny things set you back and funny things help you along. Just this week something wonderful happened.

Every Monday I have the day to myself. I loll about and drink in indulgence. This last one, I was sitting in this very room having returned from my early morning yoga classes and massage. I always follow the same ritual: on the way home I stop off at the local patisserie and buy fresh ham and cheese croissants, I come straight in and make myself a steaming pot of black coffee – one with brown bubbles swirling around the top which always portends a good brew. The house is always quiet. Brenda is pottering and Jemima and Harry are off and absorbed by school. It is a time I love.

This morning I was comfortably reading the papers although it was sheeting down with rain outside. It poured out of the sky like it does in a child's painting – vertical pencil lines coming from the bottom of low clouds. There was a fine spray along the top of the garden wall where it clattered against an unyielding surface and turned into a mist of tiny airborne droplets.

I then realised with some concern that the young couple who help us with our garden were outside and taking refuge under the eaves from the wet. Karina looked quite content, standing there in her T-shirt with her elbows poking out of the floppy sleeves and arms folded, reverently watching the storm with a far-away look in her eye. They were not interested, either of them, in coming inside. It wasn't cold out there and besides, their son was asleep in their car and they didn't want to be too far away.

I felt a prick of anxiety. Would I be so concerned? Did they feel they had to be extra vigilant? Did they sense that their fate might be tarnished by our bad luck because they were within our orbit? I dismissed such feelings. Silly. They had been with us and our children many times – only never before when theirs was sleeping.

I came inside and left them. Pretty soon the rain stopped and they were leaving. They had planted a wisteria vine for us, to replace eventually the shaggy old ornamental grape that chokes the upper verandah rail and sends loopy avaricious tendrils across to the lemon-scented gum and frangipani tree.

In the quiet of the after-storm, I went out to the terrace, paddling barefooted through the pools of water, to inspect the works. The wisteria looked good. A proper professional job; a small plant, about 18 inches high, bedded into a small square of earth where they had removed the paving. It was then that I noticed that another plant had been installed, at the base of another of the verandah pillars, not far away. I had forgotten we had asked for it, some time ago. It was an old-fashioned climbing rose. I was thrilled.

Later that day I was speaking to Karina on the telephone. She had rung me to give me the diagnosis of a disease that was devouring our azaleas and turning the leaves a flinty green. I asked her about the rose. What sort was it? How high would it grow? What was the flower like? I was caught with a thump in the chest when she told me it was called 'New Dawn'. She was not to know that Scarlett, our new-born, sleeps up there. And there was this sturdy little rose, planted at the base of her bedroom, looking for all the world like the beginnings of Jack's beanstalk.

Ever since the beginning with Scarlett, I have been looking for the sign. Something to tell me that she will survive. She is not yet two years old – and they still die from SIDS up to that age. But surely not with these goings on afoot! Such a promising arrangement, this horticultural weather vane of destiny! A rich loamy earthen base for nurturing, and a sturdy stainless steel wire to help it up the wall. The wire, particularly, takes my attention. Sort of glintingly efficient and indomitable. Absolutely taut and straight as it scales the wall. The couplings which link it to the screws in the mortar, you rotate to tighten the wire. These are a masterful feat of stream-lined gadgetry. They give the venture an air of certain viability; as if all will not pull out or blow down at the first opportunity. You can tighten the wire in the passage of time, as the pulling and thrusting of the growing plant stretches the wire and makes it slacken on the wall. And in so doing, the gulf is breached between progress and foundation.

The rose is reputed to be a prolific grower. Greatly suited to our climate and conditions, it climbs heathily and tenaciously and sends out a never-ending spray of exquisite loose-petalled pink flowers.

I have the feeling that Scarlett will survive. She won't be going anywhere – except with us.

Epilogue
October 1990

Could it be that yesterday I cleared the final hurdle?

After a three-hour meeting with Amanda, my editor at Heinemann, I found myself sitting in a brasserie in the Fulham Road in London with fresh tears springing down my face and a painful clutching of the throat which is not so familiar these days.

It is a pleasant place that brasserie. It has squeaky wooden floors and well spaced tables and you can actually sit there alone without feeling too conspicuous, even if you're crying.

I was in London for one day having finished an important five-week mission with my physiotherapy. Amanda and I had lunched to talk more about my book. I was nervous as we sat down in the restaurant; nervous like a student who sees a teacher enter the classroom with a pile of exam papers under her arm. I envied her detachment. The editing was complete but I didn't want to talk about it; see the mistakes. More importantly, I didn't want her to see what I saw.

Epilogue

We talked about other things, anything but. Tuscany, the wilds of Scotland from where I had just come.

Amanda has a full mouth which stretches back generously over her teeth when she smiles and her eyes go straight in. So when she said it, quickly and early in the piece, I was just about knocked off my perch: perhaps I might want to 'alter' the text a little, just to change things slightly? She felt that I ran the risk of being asked the unbearable when the book was published; there would be prying questions, perhaps even suggestions that Freddie was not very lovable.

What shattering paroxysms of pain and fear I felt. I could not look up, groaning, in speechless anguish, the inner cry of a mother accused. 'No!' I screamed. 'I can't do that!' Disturbing as the truth was, I couldn't change it. Not now.

As I sit here in my airline seat, speeding homeward along an imaginary corridor in the sky, I wonder whether it was her quiet, clear and thoughtful question that unleashed the reaction. Like the psychoanalyst who hopes that by popping the thought he will seed the process, it was she who catalysed the crucial undoing. In that clanking restaurant with people chatting away and poking food into their mouths, a trickle of blood began to ooze from the corner of my heart. 'This is my baby they're talking about!' There, I began

to feel the dawning of a tenderness and a protective-
ness that I had not known since Freddie was alive. It
was a lovely, restful, warm feeling and though I felt
shame, I felt a sobbing awakening within. Did this
mean that those arrested feelings were at last on the
move, chased by a vanquishing cloud of aroused
mother-love? From the trickle it began to gallop, gurgle
and foam. It gushed out of every pore in my body. It
suffused the room and covered the walls.

As I sat there, with a glass of wine poised at my lips,
lying back in the chair with my other hand holding my
elbow, I remembered full well the reproach I felt in
the first few minutes I held him dead. Disdain almost.
How could he? Wasn't he made of better stuff than
that? A flawed baby. Couldn't even hang on now!
Pah!

Some three and a half years later, I feel I am emerg-
ing. Those feelings are taking their leave. I am
watching, with swelling chest, as they drop away.
So easy. Cleaving away and shedding, like a damsel
floatingly dropping layer after layer of petticoat.
Removing the puff, the shroud of death, and unearth-
ing the innocent, my child, who at last I am free to
love.

A Selected List of Non-Fiction Available from Mandarin

While every effort is made to keep prices low, it is sometimes necessary to increase prices at short notice. Mandarin Paperbacks reserves the right to show new retail prices on covers which may differ from those previously advertised in the text or elsewhere.

The prices shown below were correct at the time of going to press.

All these books are available at your bookshop or newsagent, or can be ordered direct from the publisher. Just tick the titles you want and fill in the form below.

Mandarin Paperbacks, Cash Sales Department, PO Box 11, Falmouth, Cornwall TR10 9EN.

Please send cheque or postal order, no currency, for purchase price quoted and allow the following for postage and packing:

UK   80p for the first book, 20p for each additional book ordered to a maximum charge of £2.00.

BFPO   80p for the first book, 20p for each additional book.

Overseas   £1.50 for the first book, £1.00 for the second and 30p for each additional book
including Eire   thereafter.

NAME (Block letters) ....

ADDRESS ....

....

....